Should We Pray To God The Father Or Our Savior Jesus?

Biblical Keys To More Answered Prayers

Joel W. Hemphill

Trumpet Call Books
P.O. Box 656
Joelton, Tennessee 37080

Trumpet Call Books
P.O. Box 656
Joelton, TN 37080

www.thehemphills.com
www.trumpetcallbooks.com

Should We Pray To God The Father Or Our Savior Jesus?
(Biblical Keys To More Answered Prayers)
ISBN: 0-9671756-7-4

Copyright © 2009 by Joel W. Hemphill

All rights reserved

No portion of this book may be reproduced in any form

without the written permission of the publisher.

Printed in the United States of America

Cover Photo from Christ in Gethsemane (Christus in

Gethsemane), original oil painting

by Heinrich Ferdinand Hofmann 1890

Unless otherwise indicated, all Scripture taken from

the Holy Bible: King James Version.

"Scripture taken from the HOLY BIBLE. NEW
INTERNATIONAL VERSION Copyright © 1973, 1978, 1984
International Bible Society. Used by permission of Zondervan
Bible Publishers."

Photos of Joel and LaBreeska by

Bloodworth Photography and Ralph Barrett.

I am indebted to S. J. Austin for some of the

material used in Appendix A.

Acknowledgments

A very special thanks to our secretary Dawn Mansfield for her diligent work in typing and re-typing the manuscript. Thanks also to Lynsae Harkins of *Lynsae Design* for the cover artwork and design and to Nancy Carter of *Quality DigiPress* for the interior layout and design. A heart-felt *"thank you"* to those who received my first book, *"To God Be The Glory"* with open minds, and were like the Bereans who *"searched the Scriptures daily, whether those things were so" (Acts 17:11).*

Contents

Dedication 11

Chapter 1 - Learning Lessons Regarding Prayer 13

Chapter 2 - Jesus Himself Was A Man Of Prayer 29

Chapter 3 - The Protocol Of Approaching God 41

Chapter 4 - Praying To God In Jesus' Name 55

Chapter 5 - How Paul Prayed 67

Diagram - Paul Prayed To God 79

Appendix A - More About Praise 81

Appendix B - Persistence In Prayer 87

Appendix C - Jesus' Words In John Chapter Fourteen 91

Appendix D - Herd Mentality 97

About The Author 101

Advertisements Of CD's and Books 103

Should We Pray To God The Father Or Our Savior Jesus?

-Biblical Keys To More Answered Prayers-

By:
Joel W. Hemphill

"Then Jesus told his disciples a parable to show them that they should always pray and not give up" (Luke 18:1 NIV).

This book is about giving glory to God by approaching Him in prayer in the manner that He has instructed.

Dedication

This book is lovingly dedicated to my darling wife LaBreeska, whose fervent and consistent prayer life has helped to see us through many difficult places. With her beside me, I *"waited patiently for the Lord; and he inclined unto me, and heard my cry. He brought me up also out of an horrible pit, out of the miry clay, and set my feet upon a rock, and established my goings. And he hath put a new song in my mouth, even praise unto our God" (Psalm 40:1-3).*

God The Creator's Glory

*"Thus said the Lord, the Holy **One** of Israel, and his Maker. **I have made the earth**, and **created man** upon it: I, even **my hands**, have stretched out the heavens, and all their host have I commanded....and there is **no God else beside me**; a just God and a Saviour; **there is none beside me**. Look unto me, and be ye saved, all the ends of the earth: for **I am God, and there is none else**"* (Isaiah 45:11-12, 21-22).

*"I am the Lord: that is my name; and **my glory will I not give to another**"* (Isaiah 42:8).

*"**I will not give my glory unto another**"* (Isaiah 48:11).

*"And I saw another angel fly in the midst of heaven, having the everlasting gospel to preach unto them that dwell on the earth...Saying with a loud voice, **Fear God**, and **give glory to him**; for the hour of his judgement is come: and **worship him** that made heaven, and the earth, and the sea, and the fountains of waters"* (Revelation 14:6-7).

Jesus' Glory

*"....and we beheld **his glory**, the glory as of **the only begotten of the Father**"* (John 1:14).

*"The Son of Man...shall come in **his own glory"*** (Jesus speaking) *(Luke 9:26).*

*"The Son of man shall sit in the throne of **his glory*** (Jesus speaking) *(Matt. 19:28).*

*"Father...the **glory which thou gavest me**...that they may behold **my glory which thou hast given me**"* (Jesus speaking) *(John 17:21, 22, 24).*

(Christ) *verily was **foreordained** before the foundation of the world, but was manifest in these last times for you, Who by him do believe in **God**, that raised him up from the dead, and **gave him glory**;that your faith and hope might be in **God**"* (I Peter 1:20-21).

Chapter One
Learning Lessons Regarding Prayer

Jesus' disciples followed him in ministry from place to place and saw the awesome miracles that he preformed. Miracles such as turning the water into wine, the feeding of the five thousand, the healing of blind Bartimaeus and raising Lazarus from the dead. But the Bible gives no account of the disciples ever asking Jesus to teach them how to do these things. However in Luke 11:1 they did ask Jesus to teach them one thing. They had observed Jesus' prayer life and came to understand that his miracles and the power of his message came about through prayer. Thus their one request.

> *"And it came to pass that,* **as he was praying in a certain place, when he ceased**, *one of his disciples said unto him,* **Lord, teach us to pray,** *as John also taught his disciples" (Luke 11:1).*

So Jesus began to teach them lessons regarding prayer. In verses five through ten of this chapter he teaches them

Should We Pray to God the Father or Our Savior Jesus?

"importunity" ("to urge repeatedly") in prayer. In verses eleven through thirteen, using the example of the son asking for bread or fish, he teaches them of the **Father's willingness** to answer prayer. In chapter eighteen, verses one through eight, using the parable of the wronged widow, he taught them **persistence** in prayer and the **power of crying out** to God. In verses ten through fourteen of chapter eighteen, using the parable of the Pharisee and the publican, Jesus taught them **right attitude** in prayer. All of these are important keys to answered prayers, but perhaps the most important key, and the one most often missed is, **to whom do we address our prayers**? Look back to Luke chapter eleven, verse two.

> *"And he said unto them,* ***When ye pray, say, Our Father*** *which art in heaven, Hallowed be* ***thy name.*** ***Thy kingdom come.*** ***Thy will*** *be done, as in heaven, so in earth" (Luke 11:2).*

Notice, Jesus did not begin these teachings regarding prayer by telling them to pray to himself, the Son of God, but to, *"Our **Father** which art in heaven."* This is not just an isolated verse, but it clearly harmonizes with all of the other sayings of Jesus regarding to whom we should pray.

Chapter One – Learning Lessons Regarding Prayer

Consider the following passages.

> *"When thou prayest, enter into thy closet and...pray to **thy Father** which is in secret; and **thy Father** which seeth in secret shall reward thee openly...for **your Father** knoweth what things ye have need of, before ye **ask him**...therefore pray ye: **Our Father** which art in heaven" (Matt. 6:6, 8-9).*

> *"....your fruit should remain, that whatsoever ye shall **ask of the Father in my name, he** may give it you" (John 15:16).*

> *"I go to the Father. And in that day ye shall **ask me nothing**. Verily, Verily, I say unto you, Whatsoever ye shall **ask the Father in my name, he** will give it you. At that day ye shall **ask in my name**" (John 16:16, 23, 26).*

Should We Pray to God the Father or Our Savior Jesus?

> "***Your Father*** *which is in heaven* (shall) *give good things to them that* ***ask him***" *(Matt. 7:11).*

Look at the word "ask" in each of the preceding verses, and realize that Jesus is referring to asking in prayer. Jesus uses the word "ask" eight times in John chapters fourteen, fifteen and sixteen and not once is he referring to asking questions. The subject of these important discourses is clearly asking in prayer! That fact gives added importance to his words in John 16:23:

"**And in that day ye shall ask me nothing**." Note: The word "ask" in these eight instances is the Greek word "aiteo" (Strong's #154), and means "beg, call for, crave, desire, require." It in no way relates to the Greek word "punthanoma" (Strong's #4441), which is used in other places in Scripture and translated "ask," and means "to question, i.e. ascertain (information) by inquiry."

May I say at this point, we all have lost loved ones, sick friends, we live in a dying world, and Israel still does not understand who her Messiah is. We desperately need prayers answered, so **we must get this right!** Often the enemy has blinded us to the clear instructions given in

Chapter One – Learning Lessons Regarding Prayer

Scripture regarding prayer, and then caused us to blame God in our hearts when our prayers went unanswered. This was the case with those who Job spoke of, who said regarding the Almighty, *"what profit should we have if we pray unto him" (Job 21:15)?* The men of Jerusalem were described by the prophet Zephaniah as they *"that say in their heart, The Lord will not do good, neither will he do evil" (Zeph. 1:12).* But our Father delights in answering our prayers. Listen to Jesus' words.

> *"If ye...know how to give good gifts unto your children, **how much more** shall your Father which is in heaven **give good things** to them that **ask Him**" (Matt. 7:11).*

But we must pray in the right manner!

My awakening as to whom we should address our prayers began one day as I was reading in the Book of Acts, chapter four. The Apostles were arrested and brought before the council for the healing of the lame man in chapter three. After being questioned, threatened, and released they returned to the group of believers to report what had happened to them. Verse 24 says:

Should We Pray to God the Father or Our Savior Jesus?

> *"And when they heard that, they lifted up their voice **to God** with one accord, and said, **Lord, thou art God**, which hast made heaven, and earth, and the sea...Who by the mouth of thy servant David hast said, Why did the heathen rage, and the people imagine vain things? The kings of the earth stood up...**against the Lord**, and **against his Christ**"* (Messiah) *(vs. 24-26).*

They are clearly praying to the **Lord God** and referring to *"thy servant David"* and the Messianic psalm he penned in Psalm two. That psalm pertains to the heathen raging because God had set His King Messiah *"upon my holy hill of Zion."* They understood that this had been fulfilled in part by their recent experience, since *"the rulers were gathered together against the Lord* (God)*, and against his Christ"* (Jesus). Their prayer continues in verse twenty-seven.

> *"For of a truth against **thy holy child Jesus**, whom thou hast **anointed**, both Herod, and Pontius Pilate, with the Gentiles, and the people of Israel, were*

> *gathered together."* They were praying to the Lord God and referring to *"thy holy child Jesus."*

The prayer continues.

> *"And now, Lord, behold their threatenings: and grant unto thy servants, that with all boldness they may speak thy word, By stretching forth thine hand to heal; and that signs and wonders may be done by* **the name of thy holy child Jesus"** *(vs. 29-30).*

When I realized that these Apostles who had just seen Jesus ascend to heaven in Acts chapter one, did not pray to him in Acts chapter four, I was astonished! They prayed to the **Lord God** and twice mentioned *"thy holy child Jesus."* While growing up I was taught that Jesus **is** the "Lord God," and in fact for many years I taught that belief to others. I had to make some major adjustments in my theology. In and out of Scripture people have always prayed to their God. In the book of Jonah chapter one, the heathen shipmaster said to Jonah, *"O sleeper, arise, call upon thy God!"* And Jonah said *"I am a Hebrew; and I*

Should We Pray to God the Father or Our Savior Jesus?

*fear the Lord, the God of heaven, which hath made the seas and the dry land...Then Jonah prayed unto the **Lord his God** out of the fish's belly" (Jonah 1:6, 9; 2:1).*

So these Apostles prayed to the **Lord God** as Jonah did, with one notable difference. The Apostles prayed *"by the name of thy holy child Jesus."* What was the Apostles' understanding regarding the relationship between the Lord God and the man Jesus Christ with whom they had just spent three years in ministry? The answer is found in the two preceding chapters of Acts. Listen to Peter's sermon on the day of Pentecost from Acts chapter two.

> *"Ye men of Israel, hear these words; Jesus of Nazareth, **a man approved of God** among you by miracles and wonders and signs, which **God did** by him in the midst of you...Him being delivered by the determinate counsel and **foreknowledge** of God...**Whom God hath raised up**" (Acts 2:22-24).*

So to the apostle Peter, Jesus who was then in heaven was still *"a **man** approved of God,"* by whom God did *"miracles and wonders,"* and who when slain *"God hath* *raised up."* If Peter believed that Jesus is the Most High God, he gives no hint of it in these verses (or in any of his other writings). Notice Peter's confession to Jesus.

"And Peter answered and said unto him, Thou art the Christ" (Messiah) *(Mark 8:29).*

"But whom say ye that I am? Peter answering said, ***The Christ*** *(Messiah - anointed one)* ***of God"*** *(Luke 9:20).* My friend, there is a world of difference between "God," and "The Messiah of God!" Notice Peter's words in Acts 2:23: *"Him being delivered by the determinate counsel and* ***foreknowledge*** *of God."* This is *"foreknowledge,"* and not pre-existence.

This agrees with what Peter said in I Peter 1:20: Christ *"verily was* ***foreordained*** *before the foundation of the world, but was manifest* ***in these last times*** *for you, who by him do believe in* ***God****, that raised him up from the dead* *and **gave him glory**; that your faith and hope might be in **God**."* Again, *"foreordained"* by God, not pre-existent. Whose word are you going to take, Peter's, or the Nicean Council?

Peter Continues In Acts Chapter Two. David *"being a prophet, and knowing that God had sworn with an oath to him, that of the fruit of his loins, according to the flesh, he would raise up Christ* (Messiah) *to sit on his throne" (Acts 2:30).* Notice: It was **David's throne** in Jerusalem that Jesus Messiah was promised, and **not God's throne** in heaven. There is not one verse in the Bible where Jesus is promised God's throne in heaven! It is we who have done that in our doctrine.

*"And the **Lord God** shall give unto him the throne of **his father David**"* (Gabriel to Mary) *(Luke 1:32).*

Chapter One – Learning Lessons Regarding Prayer

*"To him that overcometh will I grant to sit with me in **my throne**, even as I also overcame, and am set down with my Father in **his throne**" (Rev. 3:21).*

Peter continues regarding David and Christ.

*"He, seeing this before, spoke of the resurrection of Christ, that his soul was not **left in hell**, neither his flesh did see corruption. This Jesus hath **God raised up**...Therefore being by the **right hand of God** exalted, and having received **of the Father** the promise of the Holy Ghost, he* (Christ) *hath shed forth this, which ye now see and hear. He* (David) *saith himself, **The Lord** said unto **my Lord**, Sit thou on my right hand, until I make thy foes thy footstool. Therefore let all the house of Israel know assuredly, that **God hath made** that same Jesus, whom ye have crucified, both **Lord** and Christ"* (Acts 2:31-36). Notice: *"God hath made that same Jesus...Lord* (Master) *and Christ"* (Messiah).

Should We Pray to God the Father or Our Savior Jesus?

Peter knew what every Christian should know, that in Scripture there are clearly two Lord's spoken of; **our heavenly Father** *"the Lord God,"* and **our Messiah** *"the Lord Jesus Christ."*

> *"The **Lord** said unto my **Lord**" (Ps. 110:1).*

> *"...denying the only **Lord God**, and our **Lord Jesus Christ**" (Jude v. 4).*

> *"**One Lord**, one faith, one baptism, **one God**, and **Father** of all" (Eph. 4:5-6).*

Now to Peter's Sermon in Acts Chapter Three.

After the healing of the lame man at the Temple a large crowd gathered wondering by what power this had been done. Peter then preached a sermon similar to the one he had preached to the multitude at Pentecost in Acts chapter two.

> *"The God of Abraham, and of Isaac, and of Jacob, **the God of our fathers**, hath glorified his Son Jesus; whom ye delivered up" (Acts 3:13).*

Chapter One – Learning Lessons Regarding Prayer

Peter made a clear distinction between the *"God of Abraham, Isaac, and Jacob, the God of our Fathers"* and *"his Son Jesus."* Why do so many misguided Christians insist on combining the two?

> *"And killed the **Prince of life**, whom **God** hath raised from the dead" (v. 15).*

Mistaken theology has made Jesus the King of the universe but Peter and the other Bible writers say he is a Prince.

- *"Messiah, the **Prince**" (Dan. 9:25).*
- *"The **Prince** of Peace" (Isa. 9:6).*
- *"The **Prince** of Life" (Acts 3:15).*
- *"A **Prince** and a Savior" (Acts 5:31).*
- *"The **Prince** of the **kings of the earth**" (Rev. 1:5).*

God Almighty is the Supreme ruler, the great King of the universe, and His Son *"the Prince,"* is under Him. *"The head of Christ is God"* (I Cor. 11:3). *"Christ is God's"* (I Cor. 3:23).

> *"Shout unto **God** with the voice of triumph. For the **Lord most high** is terrible; he is a **great King** over all the earth" (Ps. 47:2). (See also Ps. 68:24; 74:12; Dan. 2:47, 4:37; Matt. 5:35).*

Peter Continues.

"Repent ye therefore, and be converted, that your sins may be blotted out, when the times of refreshing shall come from the presence of the Lord (God)*; And **he** *(God)* **shall send Jesus Christ**, *which before was preached unto you: Whom the heavens must receive until the time of restitution of all things, which* **God hath spoken** *by the mouth of all his holy prophets since the world began" (Acts 3:19-21).* Listen to Peter! The God who sent Jesus Christ the first time has promised to send him again at *"the time of restitution of all things."* This is not God sending a "second God," this is the Lord God sending His Son, *"**the man Christ Jesus**."* To Peter and the other Apostles, in fact Jesus himself has a God.

> *"Blessed be **the God** and Father **of our** Lord Jesus Christ" (I Peter 1:3).*

> *"Blessed be **the God** and Father **of our** Lord Jesus Christ" (Eph. 1:3).*

Now to Peter's words in verses 22, 23, and 26 of Acts chapter three.

> *"For Moses truly said unto the fathers, **a Prophet** shall the **Lord** your **God** raise up*

Chapter One – Learning Lessons Regarding Prayer

*unto you **of your brethren**, like unto me* (a prophet like Moses); *him shall ye hear....and it shall come to pass, that every soul which will not hear **that Prophet**, shall be destroyed from among the people. Unto you first **God**, having raised up his Son Jesus, **sent him** to bless you" (Acts 3:22-23, 26).*

No wonder these apostles who had spent three years with Jesus in ministry, did not pray to him in Acts chapter four. To them he was the righteous sacrifice for the sins of the whole world; Messiah, Prince, and a Prophet like Moses sent by God, but he was not himself God. So they prayed to the one who is their God and ours, *("Lord, thou art God, which has made heaven and earth")*, in *"the name of thy holy child Jesus."* We desperately need to learn from their example! We have come to the end of the age and we need prayers answered. Look how God showed His approval of the manner in which they prayed.

> *"And when they had prayed, the place was shaken where they were assembled*

together; and they were all filled with the Holy Ghost, and they spoke the word of God with boldness" (v. 31).

Chapter 2
Jesus Himself Was a Man of Prayer

Prayer is a declaration of dependence upon God, and Jesus prayed always. The Bible records much regarding his prayer life.

> *"And when he had sent the multitudes away, he went up into a mountain apart **to pray**" (Matt. 14:23).*

> *"Then were there brought unto him little children, that he should **put his hands on them, and pray**" (Matt. 19:13).*

> *"Then cometh Jesus with them unto a place called Gethsemane, and saith unto the disciples, Sit ye here, **while I go and pray** yonder" (Matt. 26:36).*

> *"And in the morning, rising up a great while before day, he went out, and*

departed into a solitary place, **and there he prayed**" (Mark. 1:35).

"Now when all the people were baptized, it came to pass, that Jesus also being baptized, **and praying**, the heaven was opened, and the Holy Ghost descended in a bodily shape like a dove upon him..." (Luke 3:21-22).

"And he withdrew himself into the wilderness, **and prayed**" (Luke 5:16).

"He took Peter and John and James, and went up into a mountain **to pray. And as he prayed**, the fashion of his countenance was altered, and his raiment was white and glistering (glistening)" (Luke 9:28-29).

Luke's description of Jesus' prayer in the Garden of Gethsemane shows that Jesus' prayers were not just a formality or to set a good example.

Chapter Two – Jesus Himself Was A Man Of Prayer

> *"And **being in an agony he prayed more earnestly**: and his sweat was as it were great drops of blood falling down to the ground" (Luke 22:44).*

To Whom Did Jesus Pray?

Since Jesus is our supreme example, we would do well to study the Scriptures with the question in mind, to whom did Jesus pray? Was Jesus just a body full of God (a robot if you please) as some teach, and therefore when he prayed it was *"the flesh praying to the Spirit,"* or was this a unique, perfect, sinless man who prayed to his God? (Remember his words, *"I ascend unto...**my God** and **your God**" John 20:17).* Notice these Scriptures:

> *"And it came to pass in those days, that he went into **a mountain to pray**, and continued **all night in prayer to God**" (Luke 6:12).* (Jesus prayed **"to God"**).

> *"These words spake Jesus, and **lifted up his eyes to heaven**, and said, **Father**, the hour is come; glorify thy Son, that thy Son also may glorify thee" (John 17:1).*

Should We Pray to God the Father or Our Savior Jesus?

> "Who in the days of his flesh, when he had offered up **prayers and supplications** with strong crying and tears **unto him** (God) that was able to save him from death, and was heard in that he feared" (Heb. 5:7).

Listen to Jesus' strong cry from the cross:
> "**Father, forgive them;** for they know not what they do" (Luke 23:34).

Jesus is not saying *"I forgive you,"* though he looked upon them with forgiveness, but his prayer is to God, *"Father you forgive them!"* Compare this to Paul's words in Ephesians 4:32, *"....**God** for Christ's sake hath forgiven you,"* and in Acts 20:21, *"....**repentance toward God**, and faith toward our Lord Jesus Christ."*

Jesus' closest friends knew that while he was on earth he prayed **to God** for their needs. Look at what Martha said at the tomb of her dead brother Lazarus.

> "Then said Martha unto Jesus, Lord, if thou hadst been here, my brother had not died. But I know that **even, now,**

> *whatsoever thou wilt ask God, God will give it thee"* (John 11:21-22).

And he still prays for us in heaven. The inspired writer of Hebrews says that the ministry of Jesus is a continuing ministry.

> *"But **now, hath he obtained a more excellent ministry**, by how much also he **is** the mediator of a better covenant"* (Heb. 8:6).

Part of his continuing ministry is to intercede ("entreat in favor of") for us.

> *"Wherefore he is able to save them to the uttermost that come **unto God by him**, seeing he **ever liveth** to make intercession for them"* (Heb. 7:25).

> *"Who is even at the right hand of God, who also **maketh intercession** for us"* (Rom. 8:34).

> *"....if I go not away, the Comforter will not come unto you"* (John 16:7).

> *"And **I will pray the Father**, and he shall give you another Comforter, that he may abide with you forever" (John 14:16).*

Jesus Taught The Disciples and Us To Pray To The Father.

In Matthew chapter nine we are told that *"Jesus went about all the cities and villages, teaching in their synagogues, and preaching the gospel of the kingdom, and healing every sickness and every disease among the people" (v. 35).* As he traveled about seeing the multitudes he was *"moved with compassion on them, because they fainted, and were scattered abroad, as sheep having no shepherd" (v. 36).* Jesus saw a problem and made a request of his disciples.

Jesus' Prayer Request.

> *"Pray ye therefore **the Lord of the harvest** (not himself), that **he** will send forth labourers into **his** harvest" (Matt. 9:38).*

Jesus gave a prayer request to his disciples. He is saying in the above verse, "Help me pray to God the Father about

Chapter Two – Jesus Himself Was A Man Of Prayer

this problem." (For another example of Jesus requesting prayer from his disciples see *Matthew 26:36-43).* Jesus never claimed to be "the Lord of the harvest." Notice his words in John 15:1.

> *"I am the true vine, and **my Father** is the husbandman."*

When Jesus gave the parable of the householder in Matthew twenty-one, he pictured himself as *"his son,"* the *"heir,"* who is *"sent"* by the householder (God), and slain by the wicked men. Jesus never claimed to be *"the Father"* **and** *"the Son."* It is we who have claimed both positions for him. Note: We are heirs of God **our Father** and joint heirs with Jesus Christ **our brother** *(Rom. 8:17).*

It is remarkable that there is not one occasion recorded in the Gospels where Jesus taught them (or us) to pray to himself. In fact he clearly taught otherwise, so why do millions of Christians persist in praying to Jesus. Consider his words on this subject.

> *"But thou, when thou prayest, enter into thy closet, and when thou hast shut the door, **pray to thy Father** which is in secret; and **thy Father** which seeth in*

secret shall reward thee openly. Be not ye therefore like unto them: for **your Father** *knoweth what things ye have need of, before ye* **ask him**. **After this manner therefore pray ye: Our Father** *which art in heaven, Hallowed be* **thy name**" *(Matt. 6:6, 8-9).*

"Again I say unto you, that if two of you shall agree on earth as touching any thing that they shall ask, it shall be done for them **of my Father** *which is in heaven" (Matt. 18:19).*

"If ye then, being evil, know how to give good gifts unto your children: how much more **shall your heavenly Father give the Holy Spirit to them that ask him**" *(Luke 11:13)?* Notice, *"That ask* **him***...your heavenly Father."*

"And shall not **God** *avenge his own elect, which* **cry** *day and night* **unto him**, *though* **he** *bear long with them. I tell you*

that ***he*** *will avenge them speedily" (Luke 18:7-8).*

Origen Regarding Prayer To God.

The early Greek Church father Origen *(A.D. 185-255)* made many serious mistakes in his theology but he read these clear verses and got this much right. We are to pray to the Supreme God, and Him alone. Consider these quotes from his writings.

> [1] *"Celsus* (a Roman philosopher) *forgets that he is addressing Christians, who pray* ***to God alone*** *through Jesus. For every prayer, supplication, intercession, and thanksgiving is to be sent up* ***to the Supreme God*** *through the High Priest - the living Word and.....it would not permit us to pray with confidence to anyone other than* ***to the Supreme God****, who is sufficient for all things,* ***through*** *our Savior, the Son of God.* ***We judge it improper to pray to those beings who themselves offer up prayers****. For even they themselves would prefer that we*

---

[1] *A Dictionary of Early Christian Beliefs; David W. Beroct, Ed.; Hendrickson Publishing; 1998, p. 533*

Should We Pray to God the Father or Our Savior Jesus?

> *should send up our requests **to the God to whom they pray**, rather than to send them downwards to themselves, or **to apportion our power of prayer between God and them**."*

Origen raises a good question. Why pray to Jesus, Mary, saints, or angels when we are never instructed to do so, and when in fact we have been invited into the throne room of Almighty God Himself? I would ask this of the tens of millions of people who pray to Mary, *"Is Mary more **able** to help you than God?"* *"Is Mary more **kind, compassionate, approachable** and **ready** to help than God?"* *"Is this not an insult to our heavenly Father who is far greater in these wonderful attributes than any other?"* God our Father desires our love, fellowship and prayers. Please do yourself a great favor, if you haven't already, and establish a praise and prayer relationship with Him!

> *"Seeing then that we have **a great high priest**, that is passed into the heavens, Jesus the Son of God...Let us therefore **come boldly unto the throne of grace**,*

Chapter Two – Jesus Himself Was A Man Of Prayer

that we may obtain mercy and find grace to help in time of need" (Heb. 4:14, 16).

"In whom (Christ) *we have boldness and **access** with confidence by the faith of him. For this cause I bow my knees **unto the Father** of our Lord Jesus Christ"* (Eph. 3:12, 14).

Jesus Regarding Worship

*"Ye worship ye know not what: we know what **we worship**; for salvation is of the Jews. But the hour cometh, and now is, when the **true worshipers shall worship the Father** in spirit and in truth: for **the Father seeketh such to worship him**. God is a Spirit: And they that **worship him** must **worship him** in spirit and in truth. The woman saith unto him, I know that **Messiah** cometh, which is called Christ: when he is come, he will tell us all things. Jesus saith unto her, **I that speak unto thee am he**" (John 4:22-26).*

Chapter 3
The Protocol of Approaching God

The verses at the end of the previous chapter point us to another important subject regarding prayer. That is the protocol of approaching God. When I was a very young man I learned a good lesson about protocol. An older friend of mine was on trial in Federal Court on a draft issue, and several members of our church went with him to give moral support. We visited quietly in the courtroom until just before time for the trial to begin, when to our amazement the bailiff entered and escorted everyone from the room who did not have on a coat, including me. I sat outside in the hallway during the trial pondering the protocol of being in Federal Court in the presence of a Federal judge.

In a similar vein I heard on the news recently of a group of ladies who were invited to the White House to see the President. Whether in ignorance or irreverence the news did not say, but several of the ladies showed up in flip-flops. It caused quite a stir, as you do not go into the Oval

Office to meet the President wearing flip-flops. There is a protocol. You honor the President, you honor the office. You go at his invitation, dressed properly, and acting in a proper manner.

Likewise, there is a protocol to approaching the Great King of the Universe! When the Jewish High Priest went into the Holy of Holies once a year to meet with the God of Israel, he only went after much careful preparation. There were prescribed washings, sacrifice and attire. The penalty for breaking this protocol was death. Of course we now approach a *"throne of grace"* so the penalty is not death, just **unanswered prayers**.

The Torn Veil.

In our study of Scripture we find that the problem with we humans in our dealings with God is that often we tend to be haphazard and self-willed, while the Creator is a particular God of detail. If you have forgotten what a particular God He is, you might read again in *Exodus, Leviticus, Numbers* and *Deuteronomy* the instructions God gave to Moses pertaining to His worship and service. For instance God said to Moses regarding Aaron's once-a-year entrance into the Holy of Holies, in Leviticus 16:2:

Chapter Three – The Protocol of Approaching God

*"Speak unto Aaron thy brother, that he come not at all times into the holy place **within the veil before the mercy seat**, which is upon the ark; **that he die not**: for **I will appear** in the cloud upon the mercy seat."*

Verse three says, *"Thus shall Aaron come into the holy place:,"* and then follows thirty-two verses of detailed instructions for he and all future High Priests, to enter the holy place to meet and commune with God. Notice Exodus 25:21-22:

*"And thou shalt put the mercy seat above the ark; and in the ark thou shalt put the testimony that I shall give thee. And there **I will meet with thee**, and **I will commune with thee** from above the mercy seat, from between the two cherubims which are upon the ark of the testimony...."*

God says again in Exodus 30:6:

*"And thou shalt put it before the **veil** that is by the ark of the testimony, before the*

mercy seat that is over the testimony, ***where I will meet with thee.****"*

What an awesome privilege to **meet** and **commune** with the God of the Universe. A privilege granted to one man only once a year, on the Day of Atonement, the single most important day on the Hebrew Calendar. Others were not permitted to see inside the Holy of Holies, which was shielded from view by a curtain or veil, which hung between it and the Holy place of the Tabernacle, and later the Temple, where the congregation of Israel worshiped.

Look at Exodus 26:31, 33-34:

*"And thou shalt make a **veil** of blue, and purple, and scarlet, and fine twined linen of cunning work: with cherubim shall it be made. And thou shalt hang up the **veil** under the taches, that thou mayest bring in thither within the **veil** the ark of the testimony: and the **veil** shall divide unto you between the holy place and the most holy. And thou shalt put the mercy seat upon the ark of the testimony in the most holy place."*

Chapter Three – The Protocol of Approaching God

This beautiful curtain separated the congregation from the God of Israel when He appeared above the mercy seat. Now look at the account of Jesus' death as recorded in Matthew 27:50-51.

> *"Jesus, when he had cried again with a loud voice, yielded up the ghost. And behold,* **the veil of the temple was rent** (torn) *in twain from* **the top to the bottom***; and the earth did quake, and the rocks rent."*

It seems that God sent a mighty angel to tear the *"veil of the temple from the top to the bottom"* as Jesus died on the cross, to signify that the holy place of communion with Himself was now **open to all**, through the blood of His dear Son. Consider Hebrews 10:19-22:

> *"Having therefore, brethren, boldness to enter into the* **holiest** (the throne-room of God) *by the blood of Jesus, By* **a new and living way***, which he hath consecrated for us,* **through the veil***, that is to say,* **his flesh***; And having an* **high priest** *over the house of God;* **Let us draw near** *with a*

true heart in full assurance of faith"
(Heb. 10:19-22).

The Israelites came into the presence of God with animal sacrifices, but we enter *"by a new and living way,"* that is through the blood and torn flesh of Jesus Christ, *"the Lamb of God that taketh away the sin of the world."* Jesus is the doorway to God, but we are not to stop at the door. **The object is to get to God the Father.**

> *"No man cometh **unto the Father**, but by me"* (Jesus speaking) *(John 14:6).*

> *"Wherefore he is able also to save them to the uttermost that **come unto God** by him" (Heb. 7:25).*

> *"For Christ also hath once suffered for sins, the just for the unjust, that he might **bring us to God**..." (I Peter 3:18).*

Jesus is the door, but often we have stopped at the door. Through the death of Jesus, our sinless sacrifice and substitute, we can fellowship and talk with **God**. We have access!

Chapter Three – The Protocol of Approaching God

The Privilege of Access.

There are a number of people among us who have access to political figures and those in authority. What a privilege it would be to have regular contact with the Mayor, Governor, or President. Plenty of time to converse and express your concerns regarding things he had power to fix. Of the Mayor you might request that a pot-hole be patched on your street. Of the Governor you might request a job for your brother-in-law. To the President you might express your concerns about the world situation and stress the need to support Israel. But here is great news! Through Jesus Christ our Savior we have access to the Great God of heaven!

> *"For through him we both* (Jews and Gentiles) *have **access** by one Spirit **unto the Father**" (Eph. 2:18).*

Can we freely talk with God Himself? Sure we can! Just as the High Priest had an audience with God once a year in the Holy of Holies, we can commune with God daily in prayer. Look again at Exodus 25:22.

> *"And there I will meet with thee, and I will commune with thee..."*

Webster's new Twentieth Century Dictionary says the word *commune* means "to converse; to talk together familiarly; to impart sentiments mutually; to interchange ideas or feelings," **and then it cites the above verse** *(Ex. 25:22)* **as an example**. Remember the words of the great old hymn, *"What a privilege to carry, everything **to God** in prayer."* No wonder the apostle John writes:

> *"And truly our fellowship is with the Father, and with his Son Jesus Christ"* (I John 1:3).

The Importance of Praise in Approaching God.

It would be hard to overstate the importance of worship and praise in regard to the protocol of approaching God. Look at the songs recorded in Psalm ninety-two through one-hundred. These songs or hymns were written to be sung in the Temple, or while approaching the Temple, on the Sabbath or for high religious festivals. They celebrate God's awesome majesty, righteousness and authority. These hymns of praise and worship were "songs of ascent" that were meant to bring one into the presence of Almighty God. Look closely at Psalm one-hundred.

> *"Make a joyful noise unto the Lord, all ye lands. Serve the Lord with gladness;*

Chapter Three – The Protocol of Approaching God

come before his presence with singing. Know ye that the Lord he is God: it is he that hath made us, and not we ourselves; we are his people, and the sheep of his pasture. Enter into his gates with thanksgiving, and into his courts with praise: be thankful unto him, and bless his name. For the Lord is good; his mercy is everlasting; and his truth endureth to all generations."

David Was A Praiser!

Likely there is no one in the Bible who communed with God more than the psalmist David, and though at times he failed grievously he is still called by God, *"a man after mine own heart"* *(I Sam. 13:14; Acts 13:22).* I believe there are two main reasons that David was so beloved of the Lord. (1) When he sinned, he truly repented (see his touching prayer of repentance in *Ps. 51).* (2) David spent the days of his life praising God. He was a praiser by choice! Consider the following verses.

*"I will bless the Lord **at all times**: his praise shall **continually** be in my mouth.*

O magnify the Lord with me, and let us exalt his name together" (Ps. 34:1, 3).

"I will sing of the mercies of the Lord for ever: with my mouth will I make known thy faithfulness to all generations" (Ps. 89:1).

"O come, let us sing unto the Lord: let us make a joyful noise to the rock of our salvation. **Let us come before his presence with thanksgiving**, *and make a joyful noise unto him with psalms. For the Lord is a great God, and a great King above all gods, In his hand are the deep places, of the earth: the strength of the hills is his also. The sea is his, and he made it. And his hands formed the dry land.* **O come, let us worship and bow down: let us kneel before the Lord our maker.** *For he is our God, and we are the people of his pasture, and the sheep of his hand" (Ps. 95:1-7).*

Chapter Three – The Protocol of Approaching God

"Bless the Lord, O my soul: and all that is within me, bless his holy name. Bless the Lord, O my soul, and forget not all his benefits: Who forgiveth all thine iniquities; who healeth all thy diseases; Who redeemeth thy life from destruction; who crowneth thee with loving-kindness and tender mercies; Who satisifieth thy mouth with good things; so that thy youth is renewed like the eagle's" (Ps. 103:1-5).

"Praise ye the Lord. Praise, O ye servants of the Lord, praise the name of the Lord. Blessed be the name of the Lord from this time forth and forevermore. ***From the rising of the sun unto the going down of the same the Lord's name is to be praised.*** *The Lord is high above all nations, and his glory above the heavens. Who is like unto the Lord our God, who dwelleth on high" (Ps. 113:1-5).*

> "**Seven times a day** do I praise thee because of thy righteous judgements" (Ps. 119:164).

> "I will extol thee, my God, O king; and I will bless thy name for ever and ever. **Every day will I bless thee;** and I will praise thy name for ever and ever. Great is the Lord, and greatly to be praised; and his greatness is unsearchable" (Ps. 145:1-3).

One lesson that every Christian should learn is the importance of one on one, personal praise to God. One thing that every prayer should include is an abundance of heartfelt praise and thanksgiving to our Maker. Look at Philippians 4:6:

> "....in every thing by prayer and supplication **with thanksgiving** let your requests be made known unto God."

Luke 24:52-53 tells us that after Jesus' ascension his followers *"returned to Jerusalem with great joy: And were* **continually in the temple, praising and blessing God**,"

Chapter Three – The Protocol of Approaching God

while they waited for the promise of the Holy Ghost. If we will do more "praising and blessing God" we for sure will do more **receiving!**

The late great preacher of the gospel, *Adrian Rogers* said in a sermon a few months before his death, *"I have learned the importance of praise to God to such an extent that, when I get up in the middle of the night to go to the bathroom, I lift my hands and praise God."* I have since adopted this practice myself. Perhaps King David did the same, for he says in Psalm 119:62:

> *"**At midnight I will rise to give thanks unto thee** because of thy righteous judgements."*

Should We Pray to God the Father or Our Savior Jesus?

Chapter 4
Praying To God In Jesus' Name

*"Giving thanks always for all things **unto God and the Father** in the **name of our Lord Jesus Christ**"* (Paul speaking) *(Eph. 5:20).*

The above verse brings us to a subject that is very important in our protocol to approaching God. That is, offering our prayers to God **in Jesus name**. While Jesus was here on earth with his disciples he **functioned** as God in their lives, much as Moses functioned as the God of Egypt for a time *(Ex. 4:16; 7:1)*. He protected them *(Mark 4:35-41)*, healed their sicknesses *(Matt. 8:14-15)*, and supplied their needs *(Matt. 17:24-27)*. But he taught them that God the Father is the source *(John 5:30-31; 6:32; 7:16)*. Early in Jesus' ministry he instructed the disciples to pray to the Father *(Matt. 6:6-9; Luke 11:1-2)*, but he did not tell them to pray in his name. Since a testament *(will)* is not in force until after the death of the testator *(Heb. 9:15-16)*, they were not to invoke Jesus' name in prayer to the Father until after his death on the cross. That's why his name is not included in the prayer we call *"The Lord's Prayer."* But just before his crucifixion he began to teach them something new. In John 15:15-16 he tells them:

> *"For all things that **I have heard of my Father** I have made known unto you. Ye have not chosen me, but I have chosen you....that your fruit should remain; **that whatsoever ye shall ask of the Father in my name, he may give it you**" (John 15:15-16).*

In the next chapter he teaches them more about praying **to God in his name**. He had begun to talk to them more openly about his coming death and his ascension to the Father, and they were having a hard time grasping these statements. Notice John 16:16-17:

> *"A little while, and ye shall not see me: and again, a little while, and ye shall see me, **because I go to the Father**. Then said some of his disciples among themselves, What is this that he saith unto us, A little while, and ye shall not see me:*

Chapter Four – Praying To God In Jesus' Name

and again, a little while, and ye shall see me: and, Because I go to the Father?"

Then Jesus says this about praying to the Father after he ascends and is no longer with them (John 16:23 – 29):

*"And in that day **ye shall ask me nothing**, Verily, Verily, I say unto you, **Whatsoever ye shall ask the Father in my name, he** will give it you. Hitherto have ye asked nothing **in my name**: ask, and ye shall receive, that your joy may be full."*

*"These things have I spoken unto you in proverbs: but the time cometh when I shall no more speak unto you in proverbs, but I shall **show you plainly of the Father**. **At that day** ye shall **ask in my name**: and I say not unto you, that I will pray the Father for you: **For the Father himself loveth you**, because ye have loved me, and have believed that I came out from God. I came forth from the Father, and am come into the world: again, **I leave the world, and go to the***

> **Father**. *His disciples said unto him, Lo, now speakest thou plainly, and speakest no proverb" (John 16:23-29).* Look at Jesus' words *"at that day"* in the verse above, and realize that this was to be **after he went to the Father**. Note, *"For the Father himself loveth you."* Jesus in essence is saying, *You can pray directly to the Father because He loves you as I do.* Notice, "himself" **not** "myself".

The NIV text notes say regarding verse 27: *"Christ is explaining why the disciples can come directly to the Father in prayer. It is because the disciples have loved and trusted in Jesus, and in love God will hear their requests in Jesus' name."*

No wonder in Acts chapter four, only a few days after Jesus made these statements, these same disciples prayed to *"God,"* the *"Lord,"* **in the name of** *"thy holy child Jesus"* *(Acts 4:24, 27, 30).*

Chapter Four – Praying To God In Jesus' Name

Brethren, how did we miss these clear instructions from Jesus regarding prayer **to God our Father** in **Jesus name**? I am not being critical but I hear ministers in services and on TV praying to Jesus *"in thy name,"* praying to Jesus *"in Christ's name,"* or praying to the Father, and before the prayer is over calling Him *"Jesus,"* and thanking Him for dying for us. When I consider how wrong we have been in our approach to God, I don't wonder why we have not had **more** prayers answered, I wonder how we have had **any** prayers answered!

We should go boldly to the throne of grace in the name of Jesus, through the blood of Jesus, in his righteousness and worthiness, claiming what he purchased for us on the cross *(Isa. 53:5)*. The result will be more answered prayers! I recently had lunch with two ministers, one who strongly endorses the understanding of God as taught in my first book, and one who has my book but had only scanned over it briefly. The second minister, who pastors a large Nazarene Church, was open to this truth and eager to discuss it. When the subject of prayer came up he asked, *"Brother Joel, can we pray directly to God the Father?"* I gave him Scriptures showing that we can and he rejoiced. He said, *"I have been praying to Jesus and the other day I said, 'Jesus, will you tell your Father for me how much I love Him'?"* He was delighted to learn that we can go directly to God! We returned to my office and before they left he asked if he could offer a prayer. He prayed the most beautiful and moving prayer to *"God the Father"* in the *"name of Your Son Jesus."* Count him as another Christian who has been set free by the truth.

Other Supporting Scriptures.

Since Jesus taught his disciples to pray to God the Father in his name, and since we see that they prayed in that manner in Acts chapter four, we should strengthen our understanding of this awesome truth by looking at other supporting Scriptures. One thing that speaks loudly pertaining to this manner of praying is the absence of any Biblical account of Jesus' followers praying to him **after his ascension** to the Father. This is not surprising since any such reference would be in direct contradiction to what Jesus taught them in John chapters fifteen and sixteen. The fact is that the only occasions the N.T. records of Jesus' disciples speaking to him after his ascension to the Father are, while **in the midst of visions of him**, or **in response to being spoken to by him**.

Chapter Four – Praying To God In Jesus' Name

At this point in our study, for clearer understanding of this subject, it might be helpful to look at what the dictionary says about the words **pray** and **prayer**. *Webster's New Twentieth Century Dictionary* says regarding **Pray**: "1. Originally, to beseech; to entreat; to implore: now seldom used except as the elliptical form of *I pray you*, as *pray* tell me." In this use of the word **pray** it is a plea that is made to any other person. This is the **broadest** sense of the word. But now look at the word **pray** in the **strictest** sense of the word. *Webster's* says: "to ask earnestly; to make supplication; to say prayers, **as to God**." Regarding the word "**prayer**" *Webster's* says: "humble entreaty addressed **to God**;" "a request made **to God**;" "any spiritual communion **with God**" (bolding mine). So in the strictest sense of the word, prayer is offered "to God," and again there is not a single Scriptural reference to prayer being made to Jesus after his ascension to the Father.

Did Stephen Pray To Jesus?

Look at Acts chapter seven. Some have supposed that Stephen prayed to Jesus at the time of his stoning but a closer look at this account proves otherwise. The verses in question are fifty-nine and sixty.

"*And they stoned Stephen,* ***calling upon***

Should We Pray to God the Father or Our Savior Jesus?

> **God**, *and saying, Lord Jesus, receive my spirit" (v. 59).*

In this verse Stephen is clearly **praying to his "*God,*"** and **commending his spirit to his "*Lord*** (Master) *Jesus.*" He spoke to both because in his moment of death he was looking at **both**.

> *"Behold, I see the heavens opened, and the **Son of man** standing on the right hand of **God**" (v. 56).*

In his sermon recorded in this chapter Stephen makes a clear distinction between God and Jesus. He refers to *"God"* nineteen times and not once is he speaking of Jesus. In verse two, **God** is the *"God of glory,"* in verse thirty-two, **He** is the *"God of Abraham, Isaac, and Jacob,"* and in verse forty-eight, **He** is the *"Most High"* God. Stephen refers to **Jesus** in verse thirty-seven as *"a Prophet"* which *"the Lord your God shall raise up unto you of your brethren."* In verse fifty-two **Jesus** is the *"Just One; of whom ye have been now the betrayers and murderers."* So Stephen distinguishes between God and Jesus and gives no hint that to him they are one and the same person. Now look at verse sixty.

Chapter Four – Praying To God In Jesus' Name

> *"And he kneeled down, and cried with a loud voice, Lord, lay not this sin to their charge."*

Now the question, to whom does the word *"Lord"* refer in this verse? Stephen says *"Lord"* five other times in this chapter when he is clearly speaking of the **Lord God**. In verses thirty to thirty-three, He is the "Lord God of Abraham, Isaac and Jacob", who spoke to Moses at the burning bush. In verse thirty-seven He is the *"Lord your God"*, who promised to send Jesus as *"a Prophet"* like Moses. In verses forty-nine and fifty he is *"the Lord,"* the Creator of all. Look at the content of Stephen's prayer in verse sixty. *"Lord, lay not this sin to their **charge**."* He is for sure speaking to the **Lord God,** for he has already said in verse seven that it is God who will **judge**. This agrees with Paul's statement in Acts chapter seventeen, verse thirty-one that God *"will judge the world in righteousness,"* and Hebrews twelve, twenty-three that calls God the *"Judge of all."* Notice the similarity between Stephen's prayer and Paul's statement in Romans 8:33.

> *"Who shall lay anything to the **charge** of God's elect? It is **God** that justified."*

Should We Pray to God the Father or Our Savior Jesus?

So Stephen prayed to the *"Lord"* God that this awful sin not be laid to their charge, because he knew that the day would come when *"the dead, small and great, shall **stand before God**,"* and the books will be opened *(Rev. 20:12).*

Did John Pray To Jesus In Revelation Chapter Twenty-Two?

Another place in Scripture where some suppose they see a prayer to Jesus after his ascension to heaven, is John the Revelator's words to Jesus in Revelation 22:20, *"Amen. Even so, come, Lord Jesus."* But a closer look at the context in which this statement is made shows that rather than a prayer, John's words were a **response** to Jesus who was speaking to him. Look at verse sixteen.

> *"I Jesus have sent mine angel to testify unto you these things in the churches."*

And now to verse twenty.

> *"He which testifieth these things saith, Surely I come quickly."* And John's response in the same verse is: *"Amen. Even so, come, Lord Jesus."*

Chapter Four – Praying To God In Jesus' Name

The word *"Amen"* means *"so be it"* and is a term of agreement. So John's words, rather than being seen as a prayer must be seen as agreement with Jesus' statement to him, *"I come quickly."* If this is perceived as a prayer, it is a direct contradiction of Jesus' words that were recorded by John himself in John 16:23, *"And in that day **ye shall ask me nothing**,"* and John 16:26, *"**At that day** ye shall ask **in my name**."*

Did Paul Pray To Jesus At The Time Of His Conversion?

In Acts chapter nine Saul of Tarsus *(Paul)* saw the Lord Jesus in a vision and talked with him, but there is nothing in this chapter that indicates that Paul prayed to Jesus, or believed that he had had an encounter with *"God."* Consider Ananias' words to him as recorded in Acts 22:14:

> *"The God of our fathers* (Abraham, Isaac, and Jacob), *hath chosen thee, that thou shouldest know **his will**, and see the **Just One**, and shouldest hear the voice of his* (Jesus') *mouth."*

Should We Pray to God the Father or Our Savior Jesus?

Notice, *"God has chosen you to **see Jesus** (the Just One) and hear his voice."* Remember, Stephen had also called Jesus *"the Just One"* in Acts 7:52. Afterward Paul spoke of seeing **Jesus** *(I Cor. 9:1; 15:8),* but he never in any of his writings indicated that he had seen *"God."* Note Paul's **first sermon** after his Damascus road encounter.

> *"And straightway he preached Christ in the synagogues, **that he is the Son of God**"* (not God) *(Acts 9:20).*

Chapter 5
How Paul Prayed

In my book *"To God Be The Glory,"* I included a chapter titled *"How Paul Prayed."* In studying Scripture to write that chapter I found that the apostle Paul prayed thirty-four prayers in the Book of Acts and his thirteen epistles. According to the Scriptural record **not one of those prayers was prayed to** Jesus. Thirty-two times it specifically says he prayed to *"God,"* or *"the Father,"* or *"the Father of our Lord Jesus Christ."* (See page 79 of this book).

Look closely at the following verses that tell us clearly to whom Paul prayed.

> *"And at midnight **Paul and Silas prayed, and sang praises unto God**: and the prisoners heard them. (Acts 16:25).*
> They sang and prayed **to God**.

"Testifying both to the Jews, and also to the Greeks, **repentance toward God, and faith toward our Lord Jesus Christ**" *(Acts 20:21).* Notice: Our repentance should be *"toward God"* since it is He who has created us in His image, and He against whom we have sinned. *"Have mercy upon me, O **God**....against thee, thee only, have I sinned, and done this evil in **thy sight**"* (Ps. 51:1, 4). *"Then hath **God** also to the Gentiles **granted repentance** unto life"* (Acts 11:18). *"**God** for Christ's sake **hath forgiven you**"* (Eph. 4:32).

"And when he had thus spoken, he took bread, **and gave thanks to God** in presence of them all; and when he had broken it, he began to eat" *(Acts 27:35).* Notice, **"to God."**

"And from thence, when the brethren heard of us, they came to meet us as far as Appi forum, and the three taverns:

Chapter Five – How Paul Prayed

whom when Paul saw, **he thanked God, and took courage**" *(Acts 28:15).*

"He that eateth, eateth to the Lord, for **he giveth God thanks**: *and he that eateth not, to the Lord he eateth not,* **and giveth God thanks**" *(Rom. 14:6).*

"For it is written, As I live, saith **the Lord**, **every knee shall bow to me**, *and every tongue shall* **confess to God**. *So then every one of us shall give account of himself* **to God**" *(Rom. 14:11-12).*

"Now I beseech you, brethren, for the Lord Jesus Christ's sake,...that ye strive together with me in **your prayers to God** *for me" (Rom. 15:30).*

"Judge in yourselves: is it comely that a woman **pray unto God** *uncovered" (I Cor. 11:13)?*

"For he that speaketh in an unknown

*tongue, speaketh not unto men, **but unto God**" (I Cor. 14:2).*

*"....but if there be no interpreter....let him speak to himself, and **to God**" (I Cor. 14:28).*

*"Being enriched in every thing to all bountifulness, which causeth through us thanksgiving **to God**" (II Cor. 9:11).*

*"For this cause **I bow my knees unto the Father** of our Lord Jesus Christ" (Eph. 3:14).*

*"Giving thanks always for all things **unto God and the Father** in the **name of our Lord Jesus Christ**" (Eph. 5:20).*

*"I thank **my God** upon every remembrance of you, Always in **every prayer of mine** for you all **making request** with joy" (Phil. 1:3-4).*

Chapter Five – How Paul Prayed

*"Be careful for nothing; but in every thing by prayer and supplication with thanksgiving **let your requests be made known unto God**. And the peace of God, which passeth all understanding, shall keep your hearts and minds **through Christ Jesus**"* (Phil. 4:6-7).

*"But my **God** shall supply all your need according to **his riches** in glory by Christ Jesus"* (Phil. 4:19).

*"We give **thanks to God** and the **Father** of our Lord Jesus Christ, praying always for you"* (Col. 1:3).

*"Withal **praying also** for us, **that God** would open us a door of utterance, to speak the mystery of Christ"* (Col. 4:3).

*"For what **thanks** can we render **to God** again for you, for all the joy wherewith we joy for your sakes **before our God**"* (I Thess. 3:9).

> *"For this cause also* **thank we God** *without ceasing..." (II Thess. 2:13).*
>
> *"I exhort therefore, that, first of all,* **supplications, prayers, intercessions**, *and* **giving of thanks**, *be made for all men; For kings, and for all that are in authority; that we may lead a quiet and peaceable life in all godliness and honesty. For this is good and acceptable* **in the sight of God our Savior; For there is one God,** *and* **one mediator between God and men, the man Christ Jesus"** *(I Tim. 2:1-3, 5).*
>
> *"I thank* **my God**, *making mention of thee always* **in my prayers**" *(Philemon 1:4).*

I could only find two verses in all of Paul's writings that would even hint of praying to Jesus. One is I Timothy 1:12:

> *"And I thank Christ Jesus our Lord, who hath enabled me, for that he counted me faithful, putting me into the ministry."*

Chapter Five – How Paul Prayed

This verse probably denotes an attitude of the heart rather than a prayer, because he says five verses later:

> *"Now unto the **King eternal, immortal, invisible, the only wise God**, be honor and glory forever and ever. Amen."*

The *"**King eternal, immortal, invisible**"* is none other than *"the great King,"* the Lord God, God the Father, whom Paul called *"**the only wise God**."* Note the word *"invisible."* Our Lord Jesus was not invisible, he was seen by thousands.

The other is I Corinthians 1:1-2:

> *"Paul called to be an apostle of Jesus Christ **through the will of God**, and Sosthenes our brother, Unto the church of God which is at Corinth, to them that are sanctified in Christ Jesus, called to be saints, with all that in every place **call upon the name of Jesus Christ** our Lord"*

Should We Pray to God the Father or Our Savior Jesus?

The word *"call"* in verse two is *"epikaleomai"* in Greek (Strong's #1941) and means *"to entitle - to invoke,"* or to *"call forth."* Jesus for sure has entitled believers to *"invoke,"* or *"call forth"* his name in water baptism and in prayer. Regarding water baptism compare Luke 24:47 with Acts 2:38.

> *"And that **repentance** and **remission of sins** should be preached **in his name** among all nations, beginning at Jerusalem"* (Jesus speaking) *(Luke 24:47).*

> *"Then Peter said unto them, **Repent**, and be baptized every one of you **in the name of Jesus Christ** for the **remission of sins**...." (Acts 2:38).*

Regarding invoking Jesus' name in prayer consider his words in Mark 16:17-18:

> *"**In my name** shall they cast out devils....they shall lay hands on the sick, and they shall recover."*

Chapter Five – How Paul Prayed

So the apostle Paul addressed I Corinthians 1:2 to *"all that in every place invoke the name of Jesus Christ."* Look at the clear distinction Paul made in the following two verses.

*"Grace be unto you, and peace, from **God our Father**, and from **the Lord Jesus Christ**. I thank my God always on your behalf....."* (I Cor. 1:3-4).

More Supporting Scriptures.

Since most of us in Christianity have missed it so badly in the past as to whom we should pray, we need to look at more supporting Scriptures as we close this study.

*"...but if any man be **a worshiper of God**, and doeth his will, **him he heareth**"* (John 9:31).

*"Repent therefore of this thy wickedness, and **pray God**, if perhaps the thought of thine heart may be forgiven thee"* (Philip to Simon the Sorcerer) *(Acts 8:22).*

*"For they heard them speak with tongues, and **magnify God**" (Acts 10:46).*

"*If any of you lack wisdom, **let him ask of God**, that giveth to all men liberally and it shall be given him*" (James 1:5).

"*Every good gift and every perfect gift is from above, and cometh down from the **Father** of lights, with whom is no variableness, neither shadow of turning*" (James 1:17).

"*Therewith **bless we God**, even the **Father***" (James 3:9).

"*And if ye **call on the Father**, who without respect of persons judgeth according to every man's work...*" (I Peter 1:17).

"*Ye also...offer up spiritual sacrifices, acceptable **to God** by **Jesus Christ***" (I Peter 2:5).

Chapter Five – How Paul Prayed

In Conclusion

Since the preceding verses clearly teach us that the Apostles' view of prayer was that it should be offered to **God the Father**, and since the Bible is clearly void of any reference to a prayer offered to Jesus after his ascension, we must begin to pray in this manner. But you may say, "I have had many prayers answered that were prayed to Jesus." And I would reply, "So have we." We, along with our family and friends, have seen miracles of salvation and provision through prayers prayed to Jesus. We have seen people healed of cancer, heart trouble, asthma, Crohn's disease, shingles, and various other sicknesses and diseases through prayer to Jesus. But this is only a testimony to **God the Father's** loving patience with our lack of understanding of Scripture. May I remind you that we do not get our doctrine from our experience, but we must get our doctrine from God's Holy Bible and adjust our experience accordingly. I believe that as the light of this truth shines upon us, God the Father will require us to approach Him in the manner that He has prescribed, in order to see our prayers answered. And why shouldn't we pray to God the Father when James said:

Should We Pray to God the Father or Our Savior Jesus?

> "Every good gift and every perfect gift is from above, and **cometh down from the Father**" *(James 1:17).*

And Paul said:

> "But **my God** shall supply all your need according to **his riches** in glory **by Christ Jesus**" *(Phil. 4:19).*

Glory to God in the highest!

Paul Prayed To God

Location of Prayer in Scripture	To Whom it was Addresses
Acts 16:25	"God"
Acts 27:35	"God"
Acts 28:15	"God"
Romans 1:9-10	"God"
Romans 10:1	"God"
Romans 15:5-6	"God"
Romans 15:13	"God"
Romans 15:30	"God"
Romans 16:25-27	"God"
I Corinthians 1:4-9	"God"
II Corinthians 1:3-5	"God even the Father"
II Corinthians 2:14	"God"
II Corinthians 9:12-15	"God"
II Corinthians 13:7-9	"God"
Ephesians 1:15-23	"God"
Ephesians 3:14-21	"the Father of our Lord Jesus Christ"
Philippians 1:9-11	"God"
Philippians 4:20	"God our Father"
Colossians 1:9-12	"the Father" (God)
I Thessalonians 1:2-4	"God"
I Thessalonians 2:13	"God"
I Thessalonians 3:11-13	"God"
I Thessalonians 5:23-24	"God"
II Thessalonians 1:11-12	"God"
II Thessalonians 2:13-17	"God"
II Thessalonians 3:5	"the Lord…God"
II Thessalonians 3:16	"the Lord of peace"
I Timothy 1:17	"God"
I Timothy 6:13-17	"God" "whom no man hath seen"
II Timothy 1:3	"God"
II Timothy 1:16-18	"The Lord" (God)
II Timothy 4:14-18	"God"
Philemon 4-6	"God"

(For the answer as to why none of these prayers were addressed to Jesus, notice Paul's first sermon after his conversion on the Damascus Road. *"And immediately he preached Christ in the synagogues, that he is the **Son of God**"* Acts 9:20).

Should We Pray to God the Father or Our Savior Jesus?

Appendix A

More About Praise

In the interest of a better understanding of **praise** in Scripture and how we are called upon to worship God, I would like to call your attention to *nine* different Hebrew words that are all translated *"praise"* in the King James Version of the Bible. Again, **these words are not the same in Hebrew**, and studying their individual meanings helps us know more about Biblical praise, and therefore our proper approach to God. These words are:

1. *"Yadah"* - Strong's #3034 *"to revere or worship with extended hands."*

    "I will praise (yadah) the Lord according to his righteousness: and will sing praise (yadah) to the name of the Lord most high" (Psalm 7:17).

2. *"Towdah"* - Strong's #8426 *"adoration; specifically a choir of worshippers."*

    "....I went with them to the house of God, with the voice of joy and praise (towdah), with a multitude that kept holy day" (Psalm 42:4).

3. *"Hilluwl"* - Strong's #1974 *"rejoicing; a celebration of thanksgiving for harvest."*

   *"But in the fourth year all the fruit thereof shall be holy to **praise** (hilluwl) the Lord" (Leviticus 19:24).*

4. *"Theillah"* - Strong's #1816 *"laudation; specifically a hymn."*

   *"But thou art holy, O thou that inhabitest the **praises** (theillah) of Israel" (Psalm 22:3).*

5. *"Barak"* - Strong's #1288 *"to kneel; to bless God as a act of adoration."*

   *"**Praise** (barak) ye the Lord for the avenging of Israel" (Judges 5:2).*

6. *"Zamar"* - Strong's #2167 *"to touch the strings or parts of a musical instrument - play upon it; to make music, accompanied by the voice; hence to celebrate in song and music - sing forth praises."*

   *"My heart is fixed, O God, my heart is fixed: I will sing and give **praise** (zamar)" (Psalm 57:7).*

7. *"Shabach"* - Strong's #7623 *"to address in a loud tone - specifically loud."*

*"Because thy loving-kindness is better than life, my lips shall **praise** (shabach) thee" (Psalm 63:3).*

8. **"Shebach"** - Strong's #7624 ***"to adulate - adore - praise."***

    *"I thank thee, and **praise** (shebach) thee, O thou God of my fathers"* (Daniel's prayer) *(Daniel 2:23).*

9. **"Halal"** - Strong's #1984 ***"to shine; hence to make a show, to boast; and thus to be clamorously foolish; to rave; to celebrate."***

    *"**Praise** (halal) ye the Lord, **Praise** God in his sanctuary; **praise** him in the firmament of his power. **Praise** him for his mighty acts: **praise** him according to his excellent greatness. **Praise** him with the sound of the trumpet: **praise** him with the psaltery and harp. **Praise** him with the timbrel and dance: **praise** him with stringed instruments and organs. **Praise** him upon the loud cymbals: **Praise** him upon the high sounding cymbals. Let every thing that hath breath **praise** the Lord. **Praise** ye the Lord"* (Psalm 150:1-6).

Should We Pray to God the Father or Our Savior Jesus?

Note: The word *"praise"* in each of the above verses is *"halal"* or "**Hallelujah**" and should be read thus:
> "Hallelujah (halal) ye the Lord. Hallelujah God in his sanctuary: Hallelujah him in the firmament of his power. Hallelujah him for his mighty acts......etc."

As In Heaven, So In Earth.

Notice Jesus' words in the prayer he taught his disciples, *"Thy will be done, as in heaven, so in earth,"* and realize that the ultimate praise that God could be given on earth, is the praise He is given in heaven. How does the host of heaven praise the Eternal God? For the answer to that question lets go to the Book of Revelation.

> *"And the four beasts had each of them six wings about him; and they were full of eyes within:* **and they rest not day and night, saying, Holy, holy, holy, LORD God Almighty**, *which was, and is, and is to come. And when those beasts* **give glory and honor and thanks** *to him that sat on the throne, who liveth for ever and ever, The four and twenty elders* **fall down before him** *that sat on the throne, and* **worship** *him that liveth for ever and ever, and cast their crowns before the*

Appendix A

throne, saying, Thou art worthy, O Lord, to receive glory and honor and power: for thou hast created all things, and for thy pleasure they are and were created" (Rev. 4:8-11).

"After this I beheld, and, lo, a great multitude, which no man could number, of all nations, and kindreds, and people, and tongues, stood before the throne, and before the Lamb, clothed with white robes, and palms in their hands; ***And cried with a loud voice****, saying, Salvation to our* ***God*** *which sitteth upon the throne, and unto the Lamb. And all the* ***angels*** *stood round about the throne, and about the elders and the four beasts, and* ***fell before the throne on their faces****, and* ***worshiped God****, Saying, Amen: Blessing, and glory, and wisdom, and thanksgiving, and honor, and power, and might, be unto our* ***God*** *for ever and ever. Amen" (Rev. 7:9-12).*

"And the four and twenty elders, which sat before ***God*** *on their seats,* ***fell upon their faces, and worshiped God****, Saying,*

We give thee thanks, O Lord God Almighty, which art, and wast, and art to come; because thou hast taken to thee thy great power, and hast reigned" *(Rev. 11:16-17).*

"And I saw....them that had gotten the victory over the beast, and over his image, and over his mark, and over the number of his name, stand on the sea of glass, having the **harps** *of God.* ***And they sing*** *the song of Moses the servant of God, and the song of the Lamb, saying, Great and marvelous are thy works,* ***Lord God Almighty****; just and true are thy ways, thou King of saints. Who shall not fear thee, O Lord, and glorify thy name? for thou only art holy: for* ***all nations shall come and worship before thee"*** *(Rev. 15:2-4).*

Glory to God in the Highest!

Appendix B

Persistence In Prayer

"I have set watchmen upon thy walls, O Jerusalem, which shall never hold their peace day nor night: ye that make mention of the **Lord**, **keep not silence**. *And* **give him no rest**, *till he establish, and till he make Jerusalem a praise in the earth" (Isa. 62:6-7).*

And it came to pass in process of time, that the king of Egypt died: and the children of Israel **sighed** *by reason of the bondage, and they* **cried**, *and* **their cry came up unto God** *by reason of the bondage. And* **God heard their groaning**, *and God remembered his covenant with Abraham, with Isaac, and with Jacob. And God looked upon the children of Israel, and God had respect unto them" (Ex. 2:23-25).*

"And the Lord said, Hear what the unjust judge saith. And shall not God avenge

his own elect, **which cry day and night unto him,** *though he bear long with them"* (Jesus speaking) *(Luke 18:6-7)?*

"And being in an agony he (Jesus) ***prayed more earnestly****: and his sweat was as it were great drops of blood falling down to the ground" (Luke 22:44).*

"He (Jesus) *went away **again the second time**, and prayed, saying, O my Father, if this cup may not pass away from me, except I drink it, thy will be done. And he came and found them asleep again: for their eyes were heavy. And he left them, and went away again, and **prayed the third time, saying the same words**" (Matt. 25:42-44).* Jesus had already prayed a similar prayer several days before: *"Now is my soul troubled; and what shall I say?* **Father save me from this hour***: but for this cause came I unto this hour" (John 12:27).*

"Who in the days of his flesh, when he (Jesus) *had **offered up prayers and***

Appendix B

supplications* with *strong crying and tears *unto him that was able to save him from death, and was heard in that he feared; Though he were a Son,* ***yet learned he obedience*** *by the things which he suffered; And* ***being made perfect, he became*** *the author of eternal salvation unto all them that obey him; Called of God an high priest..." (Heb. 5:7-10).*

Should We Pray to God the Father or Our Savior Jesus?

Appendix C

Jesus' Words In John Chapter Fourteen

In studying the gospel of John, chapters fourteen, fifteen and sixteen it is clear that there is a progression in Jesus' teachings regarding his relationship with his Father, and regarding praying to the Father in Jesus name. This was near the end of his earthly ministry and it was time for his disciples to understand that he was going to the Father, and what their relationship would be with the Father and with Jesus himself after his departure. He promised to speak plainly to them of these matters *(John 16:25),* and did so until their response was:

> *"Lo, now speakest thou plainly, and speakest no proverb"* (or parable) *(John 16:29).*

According to Scripture, Jesus' first mention of praying **in his name** was in John 14:13-14:

> *"And whatsoever ye shall ask in my name, that will I do, that the Father may be glorified in the Son. If ye shall ask any thing in my name I will do it."*

Should We Pray to God the Father or Our Savior Jesus?

The words *"that will I do"* and *"I will do it"* mean **Jesus will act as God's agent in answering prayer**. The Biblical teaching regarding men and angels acting as God's agents has been little understood by many Christians. Jesus acted as God's agent in the forgiveness of sins when he said to the man sick of the palsy in Matthew 9:2, *"Son, be of good cheer; **thy sins be forgiven thee**."* After the man was healed those who saw and heard *"marveled, and **glorified God**, which had given such power unto men"* (*"men"* - Greek - *anthropos* - Strong's #444 - *"a human being - certain man"*). Note: God had not given this power to *"men,"* but to **a certain man**.

Jesus acted as God's agent in resurrection when he arose from the dead. Consider his words:

> *"I have power to lay it down* (his life), *and I have power to take it again. **This commandment have I received of my Father**" (John 10:18).* See also John 5:25-30.

Part of Jesus' on-going ministry for us before the Father is, as *"the **Apostle** and High Priest of our profession"* (Heb. 3:1). The word *"apostle"* means *"one sent forth."* Jesus was *sent* by the Father at his first coming.

Appendix C

> "*As thou hast **sent me into the world**, even so have I also **sent them into the world**"* (Jesus' prayer) *(John 17:18).*

After his ascension, Jesus was *"sent"* by the Father to intercept Saul of Tarsus (Paul) on his journey to Damascus.

> *"The **God of our fathers** hath chosen thee, that thou shouldest know his will, and see that Just One* (Jesus), *and shouldest hear the voice of his* (Jesus') *mouth"* (Ananias to Saul) *(Acts 22:14).*

Later Paul himself was sent as God's agent in winning the lost to faith in Jesus Christ. Consider his words in II Corinthians 5:20.

> *"Now, then we are **ambassadors** for Christ, **as though God did beseech you by us**: we pray you **in Christ's stead**, be ye reconciled **to God**."*

According to the apostle Peter, God will send Jesus again when it is time for his second coming.

> *"And he* (God) *shall **send Jesus Christ**, which before was preached unto you: Whom the heavens must receive until the times of the restitution of all things...."* *(Acts 3:20-21).* So Jesus acts as God's

agent, His Apostle, *"one sent forth."* As God's agent, Jesus is now actively involved with the Father in the work of building his church.

A Word Of Caution.
Do not be confused by the fact that several Bible translations, the *NASB*, the *English Standard Version*, and the *Holman Christian Standard Bible* have John 14:14 written as if Jesus said:

> *"If you ask **me** anything in my name, I will do it."*

It is apparent to me that this cannot be a proper translation because it disagrees with and contradicts other clear statements of Jesus regarding praying to the Father:

> *"....whatsoever **ye shall ask of the Father** in my name, **he** may give it you"* (John 15:16).

> *"And in the that day ye shall ask me nothing. Verily, verily, I say unto you, Whatsoever **ye shall ask the Father** in my name, **he** will give it you"* (John 16:23). **What could be clearer?**

Appendix C

It does not seem likely that Jesus would have instructed his disciples to pray to himself, **in his own name.**

The *English Standard Version* and the *Holman Christian Standard Bible* cast doubt on their own translations of John 14:14 when they say in their text notes, "some manuscripts omit *me*" in this verse. The *Holman Christian Standard Bible* adds "**other manuscripts omit all of v. 14.**"

The great *Wycliffe* translation of the New Testament from A.D. 1388 has John 14:14 reading:
> "And whatsoever thing ye **ask the Father in my name**, I shall do this thing, that the Father be glorified in the Son."

This is probably closer to Jesus' actual words as it does harmonize with his other recorded statements on this subject, and is in line with all of the recorded prayers of his disciples after his departure.

However:
> "Let every man be fully persuaded in his own mind" (Romans 14:5).

Should We Pray to God the Father or Our Savior Jesus?

Appendix D

Herd Mentality

In weighing it out whether or not to embrace Biblical truth that is unpopular, or not widely seen even though it is clearly stated in Holy Scripture, please keep this in mind. **Truth is not determined by majority vote.** Many people who never take time to search out Bible truth for themselves, take comfort in the fact that they are part of a large group or denomination, and that millions of others believe as they do. This is called "herd mentality" and in religion it is dangerous. Please consider this fact: **Truth is not diminished if the whole world denies it, and error is not strengthened though millions proclaim it!**

How many people believed that a flood was coming in Noah's day? How many people understood and believed that Jesus was the promised Messiah of Israel in 32 A.D.? How many people believed that God was about to pour out the Holy Spirit on Gentiles about 41 A.D.?

- How many stayed with Jesus when he began to speak "hard" truth?

    "From that time many of his disciples went back, ***and walked no more with him****" (John 6:66).*

- How many were willing to stand up and be counted when the going got rough?

    *"Then **all the disciples forsook him, and fled**" (Matt. 25:56).*

- How popular was Paul in his call from God to preach unpopular truth?

    *"This thou knowest, that **all they which are in Asia** be turned away from me" (II Tim. 1:15).*

- How many stood with Paul when influential people withstood his gospel message?

    *"At my first answer **no man stood with me**, but **all men forsook me**: I pray God that it may not be laid to their charge. Notwithstanding the Lord stood with me, and strengthened me; that by me the preaching might be fully known, and that all the Gentiles might hear: and I was delivered out of the mouth of the lion" (II Tim. 4:16-17).*

Dare to be different for the sake of truth!

Who and what are you following? Is it tradition and denominational doctrines, **or thus saith the word of God**?

  *"Yea, let God be true, but **every man a liar**" (Paul speaking) (Romans 3:4).*

Appendix D

> "*My* **sheep** *hear my voice, and I know them,* **and they follow me**" (Jesus speaking) *(John 10:27).*

People are like sheep and many teachers, some of them well intentioned, have led millions astray in their Biblical understanding. According to an article in the *Washington Post* newspaper, a group of shepherds ate breakfast, while they watched their large flock of sheep near the village of Gevas in eastern Turkey. To their surprise one of the sheep jumped off a 45-foot cliff to its death. Then, as the stunned shepherds looked on, the rest of the flock followed. In all, 1,500 sheep mindlessly stumbled off the cliff. Thankfully, the last 1,000 were cushioned in their fall by the growing pile of those who jumped first. According to the newspaper, 450 sheep lost their lives. Herd mentality!

No wonder the apostle Paul said:
> *"Be ye followers of me,* **even as I also am of Christ**" *(I Cor. 11:1).*

And again: *"Prove all things;* **hold fast that which is good**" *(I Thess. 5:21).*

And: *"**Nevertheless, what saith the scriptures**" (Gal. 4:30)?*

Should We Pray to God the Father or Our Savior Jesus?

About The Author

Joel Hemphill.....

- Has been married to his wife LaBreeska for over fifty-one years.

- Has been a minister of Jesus Christ for fifty years.

- Has written and recorded over 300 Gospel songs.

- Along with his family has received eight Dove Awards, and has received ten Dove nominations as Song Writer of the Year.

- Has been inducted into the Southern Gospel Music Hall of Fame and the Southern Songwriters Hall of Fame.

- Has ministered in Israel, Egypt, South Africa, the U.K., Germany, Austria, Honduras and throughout North America.

- Received a revelation in Holy Scripture in 2005 regarding the One Most High God, and wrote a revolutionary book on this subject titled *"To God Be The Glory."*

- Is helping ministers of various denominations come to this Biblical understanding daily, through his books, teaching C.D's, and tracts.

Should We Pray to God the Father or Our Savior Jesus?

CD's and Books

For Music & Preaching CD's,
Books, Prayer, or additional copies
of this study please write or phone:

Joel & LaBreeska Hemphill
P.O. Box 656
Joelton, Tennessee 37080
Phone: 615/299-0848
Fax: 615/299-0849

email: jhemphill@wildblue.net

www.thehemphills.com
www.trumpetcallbooks.com

To hear Joel teach 7 - lessons on the awesome subject of
the One Most High God
go to www.trumpetcallbooks.com

Should We Pray to God the Father or Our Savior Jesus?

CD's and Books

LaBreeska Rogers Hemphill has spent her life ministering through gospel music. In the early 1950's, she traveled as a member of The Happy Goodman Family and later for twenty-five years with her immediate family, The Hemphills. The Hemphill family, LaBreeska, Joel, and their three children, Joel Jr., Trent and Carmel (Candy)--has received a total of eight Dove awards from the Gospel Music Association.

Drawing from her life and ministry experiences, LaBreeska has done an outstanding job of writing her story. This is a life changing book that has ministered hope, encouragement and comfort to many thousands of people. She is very transparent in speaking of their martial problems and the healing, as well as Joel's two year bout with severe clinical depression, and restoration.

Joel says of *"Partners In Emotion"*, "This book is a story of divine intervention and restoration, how God brought joy out of our pain, hope out of our despair and turned our test into a testimony. Thank you Darling, for telling our story."

Bill Gaither says, "Someone has said, 'If you're going to make the

Should We Pray to God the Father or Our Savior Jesus?

journey, you might as well enjoy the trip.' I don't know two people who are enjoying the trip any more than Joel and LaBreeska Hemphill. I think you'll enjoy the journey also as you experience their emotions in the pages of this book."

Zig Ziglar says, "*Partners In Emotion* is a book about faith, love and hope. It's also about overcoming adversity, patiently pursuing your dream, honoring Christ as Lord and fulfilling your commitment through obedience to Him and His calling...You'll laugh, cry, rejoice and get downright enthusiastic as you share the experiences that LaBreeska makes so personal."

Pat Boone says, "The Hemphills have been glorious staples in gospel music for decades now--and it's no wonder that the enemy of our souls would target them in vicious ways. But Jesus promised to be with us even through 'the valley of the shadow of death.'...Read this wonderful testimony and be encouraged as I have been."

Marty Stuart says, "LaBreeska Hemphill is the matriarch of one of Gospel music's royal families. *Partners In Emotion* is a tour de force that chronicles her journey from the dusty roads of the deep south to the outer banks of the promised land. In this book, she gives us a peek at some fascinating people and places. The most extraordinary of these would be...her heart.

This book is a must for your Christian library. Available from The Hemphills, Lightning Source, Inc., or wherever fine books are sold.

CD's and Books

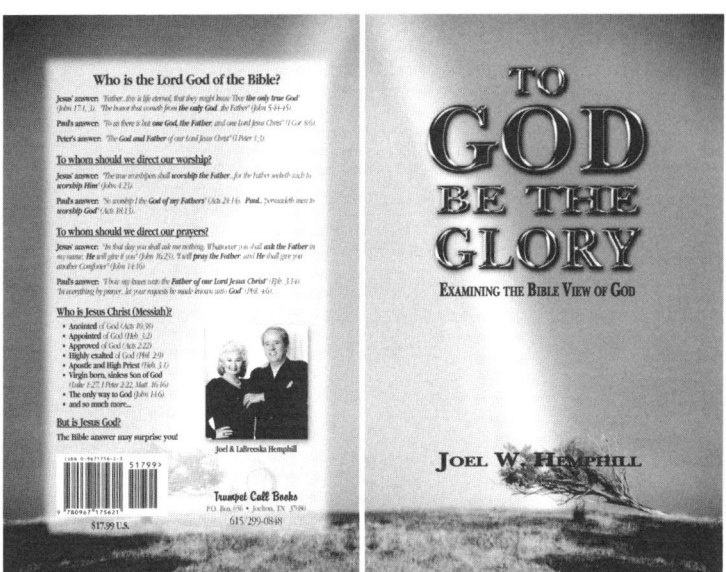

In 2006 I finished writing and published this book regarding what the Bible really teaches about the person of God. It is a 390 page book with over 1000 Scriptural references on this subject.

The reason for dealing with this issue is the great amount of confusion that there is regarding the Most High God, in relationship to His supernaturally conceived, virgin-born, sinless Son, Jesus Christ our savior and Messiah. Jesus said much on the subject of God the Father. In fact he spoke far more about his relationship with his Father than he did any other subject. He said, *"My Father is greater than I" (John 14:28)*, my Father knows things I do not know *(Matt. 24:36)*, my Father will decide who sits on my right and left in my kingdom, it *"is not mine to give" (Matt. 20:23)*, and there are things which *"the Father hath put in his own power" (Acts 1:7)*. Jesus denied being God *(Matt. 19:17)*. He denied calling himself God, with these words, *"I said I am the Son of God" (John 10:36)*. He said *"Not any man hath seen the Father" (John 6:46)*. He said the Father is *"the one and only God" (John 5:44 NASB)*, and the Father is *"the only true God" (John*

Should We Pray to God the Father or Our Savior Jesus?

17:3). He said, *"Ye seek to kill me, **a man** that hath told you the truth, which I have heard of God" (John 8:40)*. He said, *"I ascend to **my** God, and **your** God" (John 20:17)*.

The apostle Paul agreed with Jesus. He said *"**the only wise God**"* is the God who is *"**invisible**" (I Tim. 1:17)*, *"to us there is but **one God, the Father**" (I Cor. 8:6)*, and there is *"**one God and Father of all**, who is above all" (Eph. 4:6)*. He called God, *"the **God and Father** of our Lord Jesus Christ,"* and *"the **God of our Lord Jesus Christ, the Father** of glory" (Eph. 1:3,1 17)*. He said *"For this cause **I bow my knees unto the Father** of our Lord Jesus Christ,"* and give *"thanks always for all things unto God and the **Father** in the name of our Lord Jesus Christ" (Eph. 3:14; 5:20)*. Paul said at the end, Christ shall *"deliver up the kingdom **to God**, even **the Father**,"* and *"then shall the Son also himself be **subject** to him* (the Father), *that God may be all in all" (I Cor. 15:24, 28)*.

Please give this most important subject the prayerful study that it deserves.

Love in Jesus Christ,

Joel Hemphill

Joel Hemphill